Good Ol' Cowboy Stories

PAINTINGS BY

HARVEST HOUSE PUBLISHERS

EUGENE, OREGON

Good Ol' Cowboy Stories

Text copyright © 2005 by Harvest House Publishers
Eugene, Oregon 97402

Library of Congress Cataloging-in-Publication Data
Good ol' cowboy stories / paintings by Jack Terry.
     p. cm.
  Includes bibliographical references.
  ISBN-13: 978-0-7369-1625-7, ISBN-10: 07369-1625-3
  1. Cowboys—Religious life. 2. Cowboys—Anecdotes. I. Terry, Jack,
1952-
  BV4596.C65G66 2005
  636.2'13'092273—dc22

                         2005000832

Design and production by Koechel Peterson and Associates,
Minneapolis, Minnesota

"Race for a Brother's Life" is adapted from *Moving On* by Winona
Johnson Holloway (Live Oak, California: Shadow Butte Press, 1989),
p. 131. Used with permission of the author.

Quote in "Leading with Honor" is taken from *Charles Goodnight:
Cowman and Plainsman* by J. Evetts Haley (Norman: University of
Oklahoma Press, 1949).

"Love on the Range" material is taken from McKeag/Berry family stories
recorded by writer and family member Elaine Nielsen. Used with permission of the family.

"The Faith of Generations" story is based on writings in *The Great Trail
Ride* by Jack Terry (Eugene, Oregon: Harvest House Publishers, 2000).
Used with permission.

Printed in Hong Kong

07 08 09 10 11 12 / NG / 8 7 6 5 4

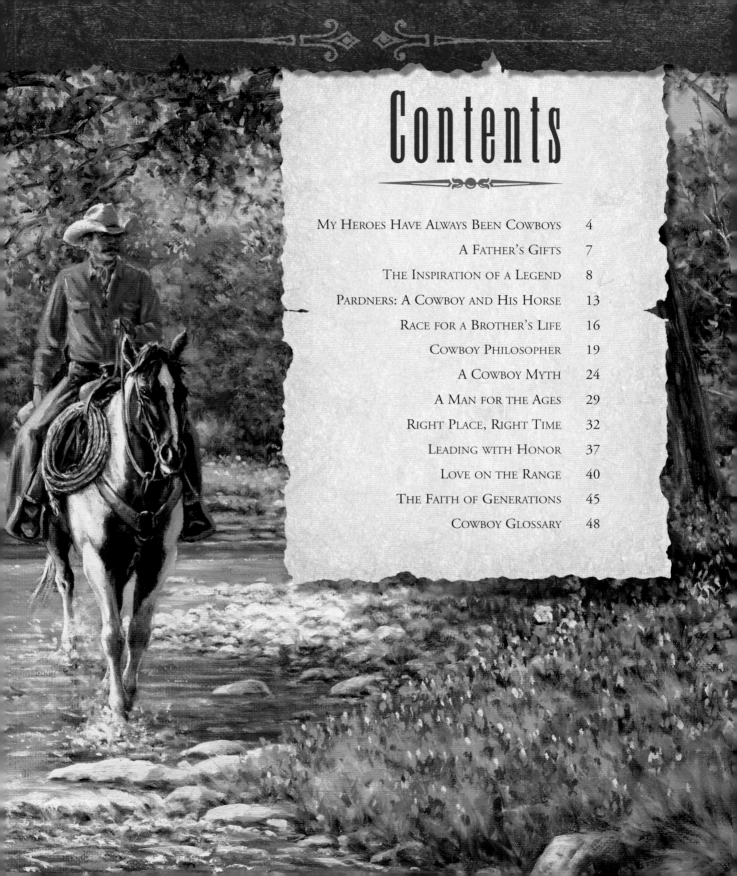

Contents

My Heroes Have Always Been Cowboys

For generations, the American cowboy has been a hero figure to people throughout the world. I know that as a child of just three, my favorite outfit was my chaps, vest, pearl-handled gun, hat, boots, and spurs. I was out to get the bad guys, and I had a badge to prove it. Even now as I sit and write, my Roy Rogers' "King of the Cowboys" pencil holder is staring at me, fully illustrated with a photo of Roy riding Trigger and the words "Smartest Horse in the Movies." While that may seem a bit childish, I can't help myself. As Willie Nelson sings, "My heroes have always been cowboys."

The cowboy way of life is deeply rooted in my family history, and it is perfectly natural for me to be drawn to that lifestyle. As I have pondered the intrigue and admiration of the cowboy by others, I am reminded of the creation of man himself. Born in the image of God, Adam was immediately faced with a battle to fight, a woman to rescue, and an adventure to wake up to every morning. As John Eldredge illustrates so well in *Wild at Heart*, a man's heart is inherently set on freedom, adventure, and a good fight between right and wrong. As society inevitably distances itself from the cowboy way of life, I contend what the world needs are more men like Bill Pickett, Roy Rogers, Charles Goodnight, John B. Stetson, Will James, Merritt Holloway, Pecos Bill, Will Rogers, Arelias Berry, and especially my grandfather, Bill Mason. All were real men who knew why they were here, where they were going, and how they were going to get there.

My granddad and the other men whose stories are told in the following pages lived by a distinct code. Their philosophy was derived from the great biblical truths. Their bond was their handshake. Right was right and wrong was wrong. Each had a job to do, and their mission was to give it their very best. The very air they breathed was a precious gift, and the things in life that deserved fighting for required their all.

Find yourself in these good ol' cowboy stories! I know you're in there somewhere.

Mother and my sisters, of course, shed a few tears; but my father, stern and unbending in his manner, gave me his benediction in these words: "Thomas Moore, you're the third son to leave our roof, but your father's blessing goes with you. I left my own home beyond the sea before I was your age." And as they all stood at the gate, I climbed into my saddle and rode away, with a lump in my throat which left me speechless to reply.

ANDY ADAMS, *DESCRIBING A YOUNG COWBOY'S DEPARTURE FOR HIS FIRST TRAIL RIDE*
THE LOG OF A COWBOY

A Father's Gifts

Born in a covered wagon in Montana, young Will James was a child of the plains and the range. With the guiding love of his parents, his first few years of life were rich with a strong sense of family and of the commitment life in the 1800s required. Tragically, he also experienced the profound sacrifice these times demanded. When he was just one year old, his mother died from the flu, leaving him and his father, Bill, to build a life alone.

Single fatherhood created many difficulties for a family. Bill had to travel for work and was often gone for weeks at a time to serve as a cowhand to break horses and round up cattle. He left young Will with good folks who were happy to have a youngster in their midst or with the trusted friend nicknamed Old-Timer, a French Canadian fur-trapper.

On one memorable return trip, Will's dad brought home a grand surprise…a perfectly-sized first saddle for Will. The even greater gift was his father's presence for a full month—a rare and precious amount of time. Father and son went on rides and enjoyed one another's company. This memory would become sacred to young Will during his growing-up years—the next job his father took would be his last.

Bill was charged and killed by an angry, injured steer. As life faded from this loving father, he told a fellow cowhand that his son was to be cared for by his confidant and devoted friend—the Old-Timer.

Will faced the loss with amazing strength, and when he was not even six years old, he and Old-Timer set out as two pardners. Though a man of few words, Old-Timer was a man of observation and kindness. He took note of Will's interest in sketching designs in the dirt, carving images on anything that stood still, reading magazine stories, and considering his own tales. One day he brought home a paper pad that opened up the world of drawing to a boy whose eye for detail and mind for story-telling later became the source of his livelihood and legacy. His stories became classics, and his book *Smoky, The Cow Horse* won the Newberry Award in 1927 and was later made into a movie three different times.

Will James was shaped by the heartache of the Western life. But he focused on a bigger lesson—those who lived on the plains and who rode the range looked out for one another. His birth-father's last act provided him with a new father…one connected by love, not blood.

Two fathers inspired one son's gifts…gifts that would later touch thousands of lives and countless generations with drawn and painted images and intriguing tales of the cowboy's sense of family pride, respect, and duty.

The Inspiration of a Legend

When his cousins came through town after months spent working the ranches and rounding-cattle, young Bill Pickett was all ears. Their tales of adventure, hard work, and cowboy camaraderie inspired his awareness of everything fantastic about the cowboy life.

Bill's father, a former slave, and his mother, Mary, had settled down near Austin to raise their thirteen children. Income was limited, so the parents depended on the help of the kids to keep their vegetable crop going and the household running. Often wandering away from the chores, Bill would steal as much time as he could to watch cattlemen in action. His fascination with this lifestyle became more than a hobby.

One day, Bill was taking notice of some of the most helpful cowhands of all…the English Bulldogs. With great interest, Bill watched a bulldog's technique for bringing down a steer. Once in proper position, a bulldog could grab the other animal's upper lip and force the bull, steer, or cow to the ground and hold it until the cowhands were able to brand or lasso it.

Thanks to bravery and a little naiveté, Bill figured that if a bulldog could do this with a large steer, then certainly he could do the same with at least a calf. After grabbing a calf by the ears initially, Bill was able to lock his teeth onto its upper lip. The grip on such a sensitive area caused the calf

to become immobilized. Bill then twisted his body and, lo and behold, he brought the calf to the ground.

Now such an amazing invention is even more thrilling if done in front of a hard-to-convince crowd. That opportunity soon materialized for Bill. While on his way to school he came across a group of cowboys having a difficult time holding down calves for branding. As the men's frustration grew, Bill's offer to help probably provided a bit of comic relief at the very least. But the seriousness of this young man turned any cynicism into curiosity…and most cowboys are bettin' men…so they gave the boy a try.

A cowboy roped one of the largest calves left to brand and told the boy to take his best shot. Bill positioned himself to bite into the calf's lip and in no time at all he signaled to the cowboys to release their hold on the animal. The experienced cowhands expected chaos, but the calf remained still until the branding was done and Bill let go.

This spark of success and respect encouraged Bill to learn all he could about riding, roping, and handling cattle and horses during his teen years. Soon he had another opportunity to create a name for himself. He "bulldogged" three wild steers in front of established, reputable cowboys

Lord, keep me safe on this trail I ride, and if sometimes I drift from Your plan,
Guide me back gently to the land that I love, with the touch of Your awesome big hand.
The stars up above, I know You named every one, and I see my name written there,
One day I'll ride home, peace and joy for my own, with not one single worry or care.

FROM "THE COWBOY'S PRAYER"

who had all but given up that very task. An invitation to a Wild West show soon followed and a career was about to be born.

The celebrity life for Bill began to unfold after he had been working on a ranch in Taylor, Texas. By then he was married, had nine children, and was a deacon in the Taylor Baptist Church. The first Taylor fair became a showcase for Bill and his brothers to show their rodeo skills. The Pickett Brothers Bronco Busters and Rough Riders were a hit. Over time, more fair jobs provided Bill with a percentage of the takings and growing popularity. At that time in history, many shows and rodeos excluded black entrants; however, Bill's fame opened doors that had seemed forever shut. Eventually, his reputation would lead to a starring role with the 101 Ranch Wild West Show.

In time, others took up bulldogging, but when Bill Pickett rode into the arenas across the United States, Mexico, England, and even South America, there was no mistaking that the audience in awe was witnessing the original. The son of a former slave became the pride of the West.

In December of 1971, 100 years after his birth, Bill Pickett was inducted into the National Rodeo Cowboy Hall of Fame. As his certificate was presented to his great-grandson, Pickett became the first black cowboy awarded a category in the National Cowboy Hall of Fame.

William "Bill" Pickett would forever be known as a great cowboy and the legend who turned his boyhood notion of bulldogging into one of the most popular and remarkable rodeo feats in history.

The cowboy became the best-known occupational type that America has given the world. He exists still and will long exist, though much changed from the original. His fame derives from the past.

J. Frank Dobie

Pardners: A Cowboy and His Horse

Hollywood presented many Western icons to the American and worldwide public. Perhaps the most well-known and beloved is Roy Rogers. Stories about Roy, his wife Dale, and their large family of adored, adopted children reflect a private man who was as noble and kind as his public persona. To this day, many hold Roy in their minds and hearts as the image of the American cowboy.

Handsome and gentle in spirit, Roy played a believable good guy on the range. Whether he broke up disputes or wooed the pretty girl—often played by real life love Dale Evans—viewers were always on his side of the fence. Real cowboys, ranchers, and rodeo professionals considered Roy's riding to be very authentic, due in part to Roy's athletic inclination. But Roy often attributed his ease in the saddle with his on and off-screen friend and partner, Trigger.

Roy's connection with Trigger was so strong right from the start that Roy did something extraordinary…he adopted him. Though he could not afford him outright, he made payments to purchase Trigger and secure him for all his future movies. Roy knew a good partner when he found him.

His instinct to buy Trigger turned out to be a very shrewd business move. When the studios were evaluating Roy's potential and value as a Western star early on, they knew that Trigger—and the very believable connection between Roy and the majestic horse—was part of that package. And the star duo became a part of film and American history.

Before his death, Trigger appeared in 83 pictures with his co-star and friend. And when they weren't filming, Trigger was a part of the Rogers family and the public's image of the cowboy life. To this day, Trigger's place in peoples' hearts is evident. As thousands of fans visit the Roy Rogers Museum, they are most drawn to the Trigger exhibit.

And just as Roy intuited that this animal was always meant to gallop with him over the open ranges and into the celluloid sunset, Western enthusiasts, movie buffs, and animal lovers know that Trigger is the ideal symbol of the partnership between a cowboy and his horse.

Without the horse what would have become of man? It has served us for transport, in agriculture, industry, and every kind of activity since the dawn of time.

BERTRAND LECLAIR

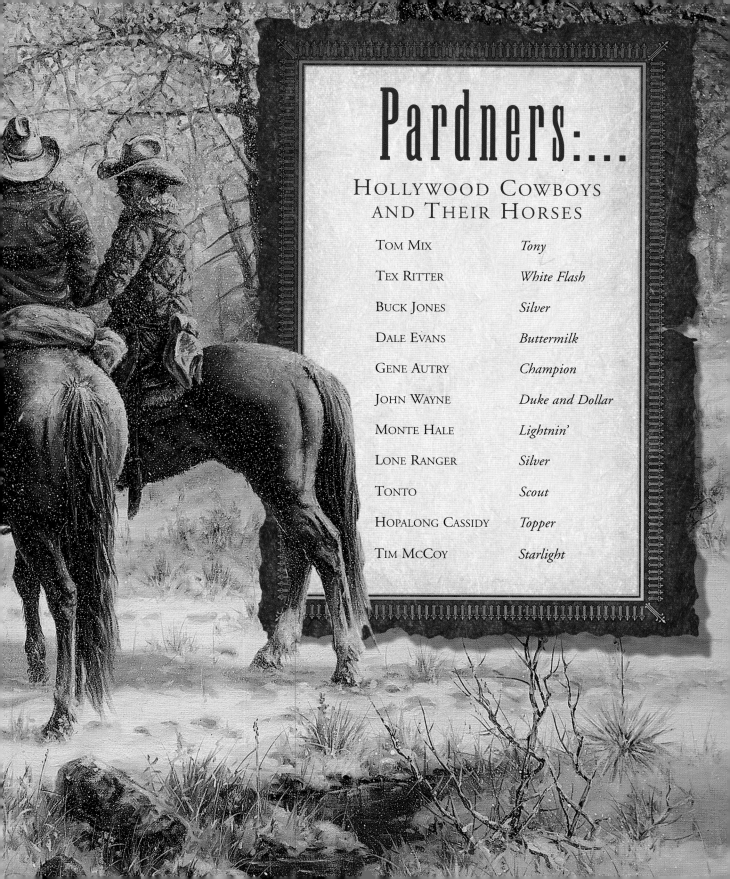

Pardners:....

HOLLYWOOD COWBOYS
AND THEIR HORSES

TOM MIX	*Tony*
TEX RITTER	*White Flash*
BUCK JONES	*Silver*
DALE EVANS	*Buttermilk*
GENE AUTRY	*Champion*
JOHN WAYNE	*Duke and Dollar*
MONTE HALE	*Lightnin'*
LONE RANGER	*Silver*
TONTO	*Scout*
HOPALONG CASSIDY	*Topper*
TIM McCOY	*Starlight*

Race for a Brother's Life

Even after there were no longer cowboys herding cattle from Texas to the West, the spirit of the cowboy was manifested in men, women, young, and old throughout the States. Many made their living as farmers and ranchers and took strong hold of the skills the cowboy had perfected.

And like the cowboys of the late 1800s, these riders of the early 1900s were aided by the speed of a good horse and inspired by the loyalty of family.

Merritt Holloway owes his life to a good horse.

In the winter of 1924 there were epidemics of both measles and scarlet fever in the country, and most children in eastern Oregon were down with one or the other. Merritt had both. He was struck with measles first and then came down with scarlet fever.

There happened to be a doctor nearby at that time who boarded at a local hotel. When Merritt's condition worsened, the doctor called out to La Grande for a serum to be sent to Enterprise on the train. It was a hard winter and the roads were bad. Automobiles were not going through. A horse could beat a sled, so it was decided that Halsey, Merritt's sixteen-year-old brother, trained like all the boys to be a wild and fearless rider, would be the one to ride out for the medicine. Merritt was in a coma and the doctor said he would be dead before morning if he was not given the serum.

This was his only chance.

And there was only one horse that could make it happen—a seven-year-old semi-outlaw who had never been tamed. Once a telephone call affirmed the medicine was in Enterprise and another rider was heading out with it on the north highway, Halsey mounted and lost no time in heading south, not sparing that wild, strong horse. He met the other rider about ten miles out of town with the medicine, turned around and rode home, a round trip of sixty miles in record time, arriving at 2:00 A.M. The doctor injected the serum and Merritt was saved.

Merritt Holloway owed his life to a doctor who knew about the life-saving serum, a mother who stayed by him night and day until he was out of danger, his brother Halsey, who was just the boy to get it back in time, and an untamed horse that could make the difficult trip.

I've always had deep faith that there is a Supreme Being, there has to be. To me that's just a normal thing to have that kind of faith. The fact that He's let me stick around a little longer, or She's let me stick around a little longer, certainly goes great with me—and I want to hang around as long as I'm healthy and not in anybody's way.

JOHN WAYNE

Cowboy Philosopher

His life began in 1879 on a ranch in the Cherokee Nation, yet Will Rogers' choices, hunger for adventure, and sincere interest in people and knowledge would take him around the world three times.

Childhood offered days of blissful time with friends who were white, black, and Indian. He was comfortable on a horse by the ripe ol' age of five and when chores were done, his time was spent riding horses or working a rope. Will's mother was forty when he was born and his brother had passed away when Will was just two…so the family knew there would be no other sons. This left Will in a position to receive extra attention and fuss from his parents and from his sisters. But soon he had to face the confines of school life and this only fueled his desire for adventure all the more. Before the natural end of his school career, Will took the initiative to ask himself to leave. He had more than 150 demerits, so a chance for redemption seemed unlikely.

Will worked on a family friend's ranch until he heard of a trail boss looking for a hand to drive a herd to Kansas. The life of a cowboy drifter started as soon as Will had a taste for rounding up cattle and taking jobs that allowed him to ride, rope, and run wild. A short stint was spent back at the family ranch but it did not have the same appeal as it did in childhood so he put more energy into entertaining folks, dancing, and singing with friends. At gatherings of new and old friends Will was often asked to speak because his humor was so entertaining. The more often this happened, the more Will realized that running the ranch was not his calling or passion. He found that being a showman put a spark in his heart that he could no longer deny.

His charm and clever lariat tricks opened doors for him with Wild West shows. But it was his quick humor and impromptu interactions with show guests and audience members that made people clamor to see him.

"I never met a man I didn't like" was a motto Will lived by. The practice of this belief made him kin to folks of all backgrounds, social levels, and political affiliations. He could hang out with cowboys and wranglers and dine with senators and presidents.

It is not enough for a man to learn how to ride; he must learn to fall.

MEXICAN PROVERB

And they all listened to him. On topics of war and peace and compassion, Will's simple language touched the hearts and influenced the perspectives of thousands of people. Every time Will returned from a trip overseas or from another part of the country, the media were eager to meet with him and quote his observations about the human condition. His humorous comments brought down barriers with laughter so that the real message of his statements could hit the mark of the listener's or reader's heart.

The cowboy code to help his fellow man influenced his life and that of others. Because he was a family man, he was not called to serve in the war, yet Will wanted to do his part. He contributed a portion of his income every month to the American Red Cross as a way to show his support. He knew the job they were doing was crucial to the survival of men and women worldwide.

The simple truths that Will Rogers shared— through Broadway and film performances, books, syndicated columns, and popular broadcasts—have worked their way into the American culture. This high school drop out became one of this century's most celebrated humorists and philosophers.

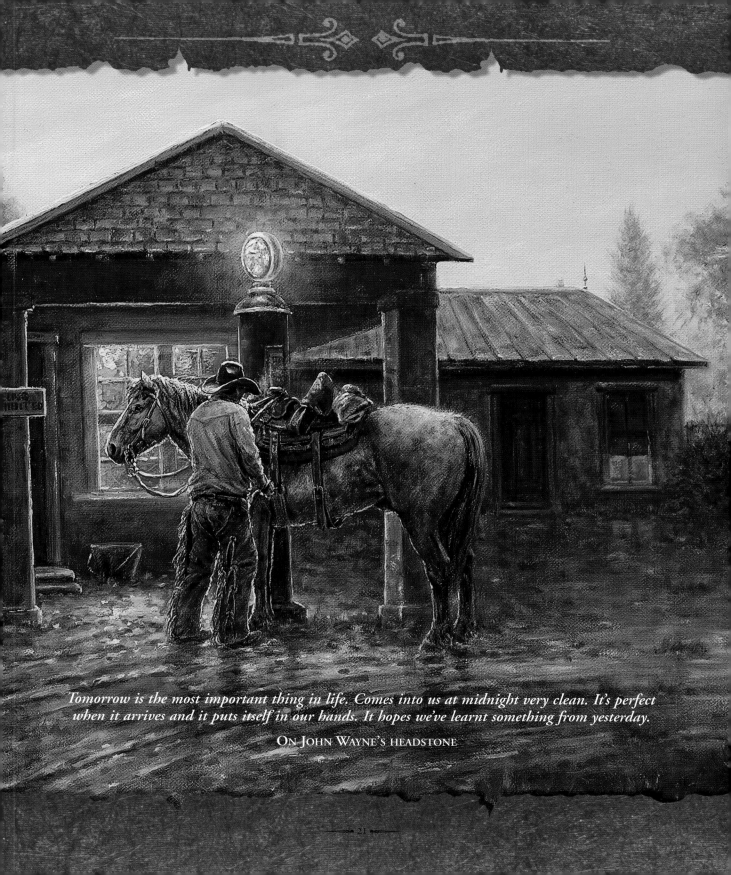

Tomorrow is the most important thing in life. Comes into us at midnight very clean. It's perfect when it arrives and it puts itself in our hands. It hopes we've learnt something from yesterday.

On John Wayne's headstone

The Wit and Wisdom of Will Rogers

My ancestors didn't come over on the Mayflower, but they were
there to meet the boat.

———◦➣◦⬡◦〜———

Live your life so that whenever you lose, you're ahead.

———◦➣◦⬡◦〜———

Even if you're on the right track, you'll get run over if you just sit there.

———◦➣◦⬡◦〜———

People talk peace. But men give their life's work to war. It won't stop 'til there is as much
brains and scientific study put to aid peace as there is to promote war.

———◦➣◦⬡◦〜———

A man that don't love a horse, there is something the matter with him.

———◦➣◦⬡◦〜———

There will never be a time when the old horse is not superior
to any auto ever made.

———◦➣◦⬡◦〜———

They may call me a rube and a hick, but I'd a lot rather be the man who bought the
Brooklyn Bridge than the man who sold it.

———◦➣◦⬡◦〜———

If you're ridin' ahead of the herd, take a look back every now and then
to make sure it's still there.

———◦➣◦⬡◦〜———

It isn't what we don't know that gives us trouble, it's what we know that ain't so.

———◦➣◦⬡◦〜———

Lord, let me live until I die.

A Cowboy Myth

A culture's folklore and myths reveal not only a lot about man's capacity for imagination but also give one a peek into the ambitions and aspirations of the people. While there are many cowboy legends told within the lineage lines of families and among inhabitants of geographic regions, the stellar cowboy myth that resonates with courage and bravado is that of Pecos Bill.

While many attribute the beginning of this folk tale to the uncorralled imagination of cowboys sitting around the fire (trying to outdo each other with giant stories and personal boasting), the foundation of this tale originated in Edward O'Reilly's story *Saga of Pecos Bill*, published in 1923.

Joining the ranks of other characters of mythical proportions and attributes like Paul Bunyan or Iron John, Pecos Bill became a popular, fictional figure in cowboy history. As with any myth, there are many versions of hyperbole that stretch and pull reason and possibility into fantastical stories that may only have a thread of the original tale told by O'Reilly. That is the personal freedom and expression a myth offers its teller. This story, shared in plays, movies, books, cartoons, and even poetry, remains a classic.

This brief version is just one of those variations. And, of course, it is positively, absolutely true.

PECOS BILL

Pecos Bill was more than a man; he had his beginning among the wild creatures of the mountains, streams, and rugged country. You see, Bill was the youngest of eighteen children born to Texas pioneer parents. On their journey, baby Bill had fallen from the covered wagon near the Pecos River. As the family continued, oblivious to the loss of their smallest, Bill was embraced and raised by coyotes from that time on. Well, Bill naturally assumed he was one of these fine creatures.

Not until many years later did Bill encounter a cowboy who convinced him that he was not a coyote but was a man…and not only that, but a man worthy of being called a "cowboy."

Pecos Bill, in his newly established humanity, became a cowhand and soon was inventing all things cowboy. His first gift to those who rode the range was the creation of a lasso. He followed that with the invention of the branding iron to prevent cattle rustling. Pecos Bill could ride like the wind…in fact, legend has it that he rode the wind in the form of a cyclone. But like any cowboy worth his saddle, his favorite ride was his horse…Widow-Maker.

His feats were not just displays of physical might and courageous gusto. With sensitivity and style he also created the cowboy song as a way to calm the cattle at night when they were restless and afraid of wild animals that lurked in the edge of darkness.

Pecos Bill makes appearances in various story versions as a buffalo hunter, oilfield worker, and railroad contractor. But the essence of his identity is all cowboy. After all, he could rope an entire herd at one go and he ingeniously used the entire Rio Grande to water his ranch. There is much dispute and controversy over the actual demise of Pecos Bill, but the way he died is of little importance. It was the way he lived…in story and mind and heart that had its irreversible influence on a culture.

Pecos Bill lived large. He was an invented man of invention. The elements of the earth and sky were his to ride and master. Bill was a character of courage, perseverance, and intuition. He could take any circumstance and turn it on its head, rope it, brand it, and without a doubt…tame it.

After all, Pecos Bill was a cowboy.

A man on a horse is spiritually, as well as physically, bigger than a man on foot.

JOHN STEINBECK

A Man for the Ages

Some cowboy legends seem like myths because the stories or the persona portrayed seems too big. One such character is Buffalo Bill Cody. His moniker came from the days when he supplied buffalo meat to railroad workers. Though this was just one of many jobs, the nickname stuck and later held significance for quite a different reason.

Those other jobs included interesting roles—a trapper, frontiersman, Pony Express Rider, a Civil War soldier, stagecoach driver, and many others. Perhaps he was one of those folks who had so many talents that it was hard to settle on any one job. He found the solution when he entered show business. He toured the United States performing plays based on his personal western adventures.

This initial tour would grow into the Buffalo Bill Wild West Show. Realizing how popular these performances and reenactments were, Bill invited big names to become part of the show. His headliners included Annie Oakley and Sitting Bull. He employed many other Indians because he felt the life he offered on the road with his show was a better one than many of them were left to live after being exploited or betrayed by the United States government. Bill's years as a scout impressed upon him a deep respect for the Native Indians and their skills, their understanding of nature and its resources, and their ways of living.

The fascination with the cowboy culture was evident in the large crowds that would gather for the successful shows during countless stops in the United States and a European tour in 1889. Stepping into the role of businessman, Buffalo Bill set up an exhibit near the 1893 Chicago World's Fair and his popularity skyrocketed.

The show would fascinate audiences for years. The country was moving from the untamed, wild West, where cowboys served a vital role in bringing cattle from the South to the midwest and beyond. The small towns that the cattleman helped establish along their trail routes had turned into growing cities or ghost towns by now. The landscape was changing, yet people desired to rekindle the passion and

No memory is ever alone; it's at the end of a trail of memories,
a dozen trails that each have their own associations.

Louis L'Amour

intensity of the cowboy lore. Buffalo Bill's Wild West Show fed that hunger.

Buffalo Bill would witness many atrocities in his lifetime…the exploitation of Indians, women, and the natural resources that once had been so abundant and spectacular. He was surprisingly outspoken about the rights of women and Indians and also about the abuse of the resources.

Perhaps the most surprising twist of all was that Buffalo Bill, who got his name from delivering buffalo meat, became one of the most outspoken supporters for protecting the buffalo…the symbol of the frontier and the wild West. Maybe he understood that like himself, the buffalo's time as an icon in the West was limited and passing quickly.

Over the years, many actors have portrayed Buffalo Bill's dimensional character…from William Fairbanks to Roy Rogers to Paul Newman. The role attracts those who want to play a colorful, larger-than-life character. In spite of the glory Buffalo Bill brought to the battles between man and nature, cowboys and Indians, he used much of his energy and passion to lift up the harmony and balance that the West embodied. His show became an effort to preserve something of what he held sacred throughout the days of his own journey.

Teach me the faith of the mountains, serene and sublime,
The deep-rooted joy of just living one day at a time;
Leaving the petty possessions the valley-folk buy
For the glory of glad wind-swept spaces where earth meets the sky.

Teach me the faith of the mountains, their strength to endure,
The breadth and the depth of their vision, unswerving and sure,
Counting the dawn and the starlight as parts of one whole
Wrought by the Spirit Eternal, within His control.

Author Unknown

Right Place, Right Time

Sometimes the road less traveled becomes a Westerner's ticket to a good life. A journey of detours played out in the life of John, a hat maker born in New Jersey in 1830. He faced trials and what seemed like an unfair amount of closed doors along the way, yet these twists of fate led him to create the most recognized symbol of the cowboy.

As was tradition, John learned his trade from his father, who was a hatter. But when his father passed away, he was left to do much of the work since his brothers preferred gathering profits over generating them. John was planning to break out on his own until he contracted tuberculosis. The dream of creating his own business would require more energy and stamina than he could muster.

Many folks who became afflicted with tuberculosis in these times headed to different climates and more open spaces to reduce the health risks. With his plans shattered, John decided to move to Missouri where he took up the trade of molding bricks. His hard work paid off and he gained more responsibility in this business. That is until the rushing, merciless waters of a flooding Missouri river washed out his inventory. He was left with nothing.

Once again, everything seemed to be going wrong for this man trying to find his own path and a good life. He tried to enlist with the army as the Civil War started up. But his weak physical condition made that impossible. He was not accepted, and his next step was uncertain. His town of St. Joseph was a trading post, so news of gold mining and trapping came through there daily. On one fortunate occasion, John spoke with a party headed to Pike's Peak to do some mining. They invited him along and the prospect of prospecting appealed to this man now without a trade.

The hard life in the mining camps might have appeared to be another unfortunate turn in John's life, but the weather soon provided him with an opportunity to turn his skill into gold. When rain storms hit, there was little way for the miners to stay dry. They would gather various animal skins together and drape them above for protection. But skins that are not prepared will soon be as leaky as cloth. Well, John knew, as a hatter, that once furs are felted, they are waterproof. So to show the other men his vision, he created a wide-brimmed hat out of felted skins. The elements would roll right off of the interesting hat that got a lot of attention. Many initially laughed at the shape and large brim—but few could refute the effectiveness of John's invention.

The story goes that John crossed paths with a Mexican bullwhacker who immediately saw the value of such a hat when out driving cattle, exposed to the burning wind and pelting rain. He gave John a five-dollar gold piece and

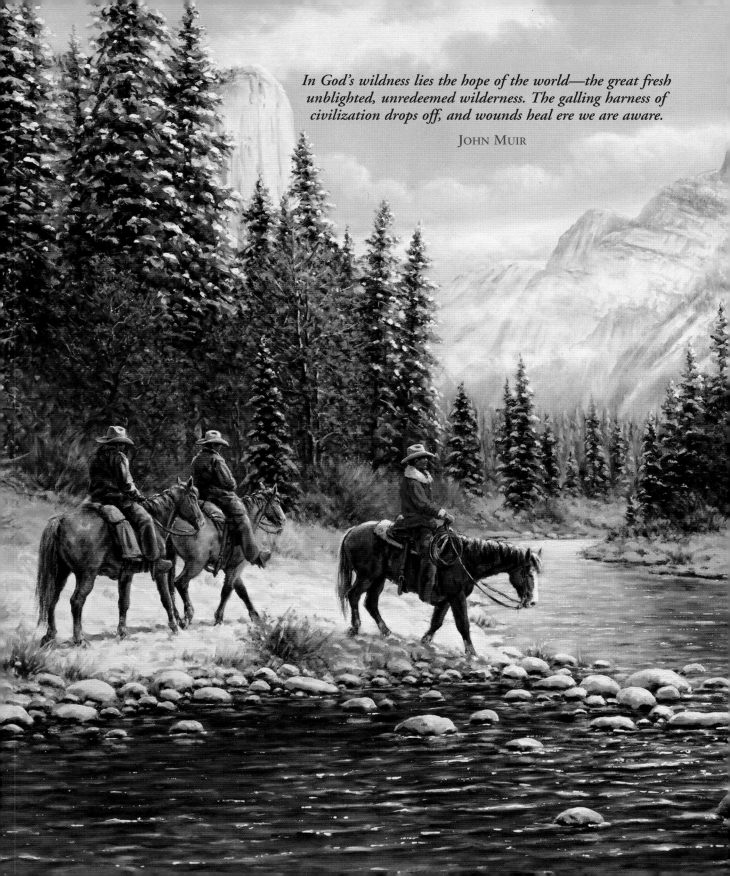

In God's wildness lies the hope of the world—the great fresh
unblighted, unredeemed wilderness. The galling harness of
civilization drops off, and wounds heal ere we are aware.

JOHN MUIR

placed the wide-brimmed creation on his head. The image of that handsome, rugged man's face shielded from the elements in this hat stuck with John. He knew he was on to something that would eventually change the look of the West.

John made a move to Philadelphia and for 100 dollars started up his own hat business. Keeping the model of the cattleman in mind, he produced what he called the "Boss of the Plains": a natural colored hat with a four inch brim and four inch top…a hat durable enough to meet the tough needs of the growing group known as cowboys. Their role in history was just beginning, and thanks to a few detours and bouts of hard luck, John Stetson's hats also became known and respected throughout the country, world, and history as the most important item a cowboy would ever own.

Eventually, any known cowboy had a Stetson on his crown…from Buffalo Bill to the famous movie cowboy Tom Mix.

When John Stetson first learned the hatting trade, little did he know that the ups and downs he faced and the perseverance he modeled would lead to a creation that not only changed the face of the West through its function, but changed the silhouette of the West with its unique, unmistakable look.

The Look of the American Cowboy

A COWBOY'S HAT WAS A WHOLE LOT MORE
THAN JUST A HAT.
IT WAS A...

Harbor from the elements

Swatter to deter flies and mosquitoes

Pillow when sleeping under the stars

Scoop to gather water for a thirsty cowboy and his horse

Prized possession for every cowboy

WHAT COWBOYS WORE

Wool long johns

Wool shirt or sometimes cavalry shirts

Leather cuffs to protect the wrist and shirt sleeves from wear

Trousers made of wool

Leather chaps

Gun belt and holster

Work boots and rowel spurs

Cotton bandana used as sun protection and as
a breathing mask on the dusty trails

A Stetson original

Some people wonder at the clothes and riggin's of the cowboy, why the silver on spurs and bit, or anything a little fancy. It seems to them that some things are useless and only for show. But the range riding cowboy has nobody around him to show off to and everything he wears is altogether for use. At the same time he can have a little style too, and an outfit to be proud of, specially when he makes his living in it and uses it three hundred and sixty days in the year....There's nothing the cowboy wears that could be near as useless as an imported necktie or a stiff collar.

WILL JAMES
from his autobiography *Lone Cowboy*

I wish I could find words to express the trueness, the loyalty to their trust and to each other of the old trail hands....I wish I could convey in language the feelings of companionship we had for one another.

CHARLES GOODNIGHT

Leading with Honor

By the time a wrangler earned his way to being a full-fledged cowboy on a roundup or cattle ride, he often possessed the qualities of a leader. He could put together a good crew of hardworking people with a variety of skills. Instinctively, he knew how to avoid dangers or unnecessary delays. Resources were valued and used wisely. And he carved out ways in these difficult times that others followed to make their journeys.

One such leader was a man named Charles Goodnight, who was a strong rider and cattleman from the very beginning. Hard work was the way of life and during the period of range development in the 1850s, dreams of fortune and success also crept into the minds and plans of young men, including Charles. He worked numerous jobs starting in his early teens to gain independence and to further his quest for adventure. Over the years, his trials on the trails prepared him to later carve out one of the most traveled and well-known cattle trails—the Goodnight-Loving Trail which stretched from Texas to Fort Sumner and then onto Cheyenne.

Even more valuable than wealth and fame were the lessons of principle and value Goodnight learned. On one particularly daunting trip early in his career, Goodnight and his men were ill, weakening each day, and had one portion of bacon between them and five hundred miles left to journey with their herd. It was in this low time that Goodnight perhaps learned the lesson that would elevate him to greater, more responsible leadership.

"I learned a lesson that I never forgot as I looked at the boys and thought to myself: 'Here you are with more gold than you ever had in your life, and it won't buy you a drink of water, and it won't get you food. For this gold you may have led three men to their death—for a thing that is utterly useless to you!' I never got over the impression it made on me, and I believe it is one reason why I have never worshipped money since."

This understanding provided Goodnight with the conviction to do right by people who were loyal to him and to never let money be his only motivation. When his dear friend Oliver Loving died in Fort Sumner after an arm amputation drained his last bit of strength, Goodnight continued to pay the proper share of earnings to his partner's family so that they would not fall into debt. And he honored his dear friend's request to return his body to his home state of Texas, the land of his youth, heritage, and family.

After his many journeys through the rugged terrain from the South to the West, Goodnight left his predecessors with more than a trail, more than a practical solution for the transportation of necessary sustenance, he left the cowboys who followed with an image of adventure, partnership, and honor that helped shape the untamed West.

The Chuck Wagon

FOOD ON THE TRAIL

One of Goodnight's big contributions to the cowboy way of life reflects his ingenuity and practicality…the prototype for the chuck wagon. Before embarking on a long trail ride, he took an old army surplus Studebaker wagon which had steel axles sturdy enough to withstand the months on the rugged trails. Goodnight knew he had a structure he could load heavily and trust to make the rocky journey. He affixed a chuck box with drawers, shelves, and space to carry all a cook's equipment and ingredients. The back of the wagon had a hinged lid that when laid out served as a counter surface for meal preparation or service.

Dutch ovens were carried in the boot and a water barrel was hooked to the side of the wagon along with other tools.

CHUCK WAGON FOOD

Learning a thing or two from his mother, Charles always took a jar of sourdough starter with him on the trail. From this, the cook or the men could whip up a batch of one of the mean mainstays…sourdough biscuits. Other favorite items to pack in a typical chuck wagon included beans, corn, black-eyed peas, bacon, and beef or bison steaks, seasonings, flour, and, of course, coffee.

CHUCK WAGON ETIQUETTE

- No one eats until Cookie calls.

- When Cookie calls, everyone comes a runnin'.

- Hungry cowboys wait for no man. They fill their plates, fill their bellies, and then move on so stragglers can fill their plates.

- Cowboys eat first, talk later.

- It's okay to eat with your fingers.

- If you're refilling the coffee cup and someone yells "Man at the pot," you're obliged to serve refills.

- Don't take the last serving unless you're sure you're the last man.

- Food left on the plate is an insult to the cook.

- No running or saddling a horse near the wagon.

- If you come across any good firewood, bring it back with you.

- Strangers are always welcome at the wagon.

AUTHOR UNKNOWN

Love on the Range

It is not easy to find true love when a man rides the trails, gathers herds from the far reaches of the land, and ventures out for months at a time with no definite plans for his return. A life of hardship made courtship nearly impossible. While the system of self-reliance practically required the help and companionship of a loyal spouse, a family's self-sufficiency and isolation made it quite difficult for young folks to meet that spouse. Many marriages took place between the young men and women of neighboring ranches, who met through social gatherings in town or when families got together to help one another during the busy labor seasons.

With so many factors working against two people meeting one another, there were times when strangers could only attribute their meeting to God's grace. Only a miracle could direct their paths, which started so many miles apart to end up converged, somehow, someway, in the same small town or in the same small circle of friends.

ARELIAS AND EDITH

Arelias Berry was a handsome, adventurous young man who took a job escorting a herd of cattle from Texas to Nebraska. His sights were set on reaching Montana after his delivery was made…and there was little to stand in his way.

But of course, he did not count on a few new offers of work and an encounter with love.

He first cast his eyes on the lovely Midwestern girl, Edith Stansbery, at the dance hall in Ogallala, Nebraska. A keen observer, he noticed that she did not seem to have a steady beau as did her equally pretty sisters. Once he knew this observation was also fact, he told a mutual friend, Gus, to "tell her she now has a beau." Cowboys rarely want for cockiness. But being sure of oneself is always such a different game than being sure of the other person. And Edith was not as immediately smitten with the young stranger.

Arelias stayed on in the general area; his exodus to Montana growing less urgent with each occasion he happened upon Edith. Soon, when he was working far away, they would exchange letters and it was evident that they both had piqued the interest of the other. Because Arelias was a strong and smart worker, he was in demand. When the big jobs requiring more distance came along, his name was usually at the top of the crew organizer's list. During one such time of travel, a would-be suitor of Edith's, Charlie, made the most of his competition's absence. While he never really stood a chance with Edith, Charlie was quick to point out how Arelias's time away must surely be a sign of his lack of true affection for her. "If he really cared for you, he'd find a way to see you."

You can imagine how this fueled the already building doubts in the heart of the vibrant and headstrong girl. After chewing on Charlie's words in private, Edith put pen to paper and created a rather scolding letter to send to her roaming crush.

To make the impact of the letter worse, Arelias had just finished fighting with one of the men in the crew. It was a bitter argument and not only was he offended, but his status as a Texan was offended as well. This was enough to get the stubborn and little bit wild young man riled up...so much so that when Edith's admonishing and hurtful words reached him, he made the decision to return to Texas. Forget Montana. Forget love. It was time to head on home.

As with any good romance story, these two stubborn lovers would cross paths before Arelias could start this trek. He returned a stray steer to his good friend Gus at the same time Edith and her family were visiting their dear friends. When Gus told Arelias Edith was inside awaiting dinner, the young man recalled the disappointing letter and said, "I don't think she wants to see me." But Gus knew better and nudged the young man to come on inside. Both men knew Arelias was longing to have a second chance with the girl. So he went.

The time that Edith and Arelias shared at that ranch was filled with awkward conversations and the avoidance of one another's eyes at the supper table. It seemed that perhaps they were both too stubborn to see through their frustration to the genuine feelings they had for one another. Those around the couple did not know whether this love story would follow the trail of heartbreak or happiness. Finally, Arelias asked Edith to go

on a walk. She quietly agreed to join him and off they went past the corral to a nearby hill. From this spot above the ranch, the two young people could see a team and wagon going towards another town. Arelias wrapped his arms around Edith and pointed to the wagon in the distance. It held his trunk, all of his possessions, and was headed for the depot and the first leg of his return journey to Texas.

Perhaps there was a lovely moon that evening, or the night air cleared their heads of petty squabbles and made room to acknowledge their true feelings...whatever happened, the two returned to Edith's home with an understanding that they were a couple. And Arelias would retrieve that trunk.

No more talk of Texas came out of Arelias's mouth. His feet, his life, and his heart all faced the same direction...toward Edith. Not long after the walk that changed the course of this couple's journey, the two were wed at a joyous celebration among family and friends. The wedding reception lasted well into the night as guests laughed and danced and rejoiced with the couple whose affection for one another was so evident.

Before it was time to go, those loved ones gathered to sing "God Be with You 'Til We Meet Again" to wish the couple well. The words of the song echoed the strength of the One who kept hope and love aflame when a young cowboy and the girl of his dreams faced the agony of time and distance apart and the hardship of the Western life. Through divine orchestration, these two did meet again...and again...until the promise of a good and loving life became a blessing they both embraced. 🐎

The Faith of Generations

After the trail work is done and supper is finished, there is a memorable moment when the cowboy lays down on the ground, eager for rest, and takes in the vastness of God's night sky. One such night during the dawn of the cowboy era, a young Texan named Bill Mason, who was on a cattle drive from South Texas to the railhead in Abilene, Kansas, felt a bit homesick. Naturally his thoughts turned toward his family—days away in distance but very near in mind and spirit. In that moment of missing, he remembered the promise made to his mother…he would not let a day go by without saying a prayer. So, he began with words he knew by heart, "Our Father who art in heaven…." Looking up at the stars, his spoken prayer turned to a time of praise as he considered the Creator of the heavenly show above.

In the back of Bill's mind, he knew there was a Scripture verse that resonated with this moment. He reached for the worn Bible in his pack and found the words in Isaiah: "Who has measured the waters in the hollow of His hand or with the breadth of his hands marked off the heavens." With reverence, Bill took in the immensity of the galaxy before him and a strong sense of God was placed on this cowboy's spirit. Over the years this belief in God's presence would shift to the back of his mind, where it would wait for a time of greater understanding.

This teen grew into a respected man and rancher. He married his sweetheart, Maggie, and became the proud father of six children. And while he honored the Creator with his humility and compassion for others, he viewed going to church as a lot of cowboys did…it was a lot of time to spend indoors when one could be out working.

But the faithful prayers of his wife over the many years would soon lead Bill to give his life over to the Lord. From that point on, he had a greater sense of purpose. The way he lived his life was a testament to this revived sense of God. Topping his list of priorities was the

Dear Lord, God in heaven, from my bedroll on the ground—
I can't help but see Your majesty in the stars sparkling all around.
Your Good Book says You have a name for every star I see above,
I know You're looking at me too, for I can feel Your love.

FROM "THE COWBOY'S PRAYER"

sharing of his life and faith lessons with his grandchildren, including Western artist and cowboy Jack Terry.

As a child, Jack thought his granddaddy was the wisest man alive. One day his grandfather shared his secret, a Bible verse he lived by, "Do not let this Book of the Law depart from your mouth; meditate on it day and night, so that you may be careful to do everything written in it. Then you will be prosperous and successful" (Joshua 1:8). This became one of Jack's favorite verses and a cornerstone for his life. It helped him define his faith and lean on it as he became a man and started his own family.

Now, decades after Bill Mason's night of contemplation under the constellations, his grandson has grandchildren of his own. And topping Jack's list of priorities is the sharing of stories about their Great-Granddaddy Bill, a man who would gladly give to a stranger in need; a man who cherished his family; a man whose word was more solid than a contract; a man who loved the land and sky; a man who lived each day with gratitude to the God he met, face to face, under the stars as a young cowboy.

Go West, young man, and grow up with the country.

HORACE GREELEY

Cowboy Glossary

BURNING DAYLIGHT	*wasting time*
CHEW IT FINE	*think it over*
SHADED-UP	*when cowboys or cattle head for rest in the shade*
HUNKER	*squatting on the heels*
GATHER	*cattle rounded up*
LARIAT	*a 40-foot rope with one end looped through an eyelet, used to capture cattle*
BEDROLL	*blankets used for sleeping that are kept rolled up while traveling*
MUSTANG	*a feral horse*
CIMARRON	*an outlaw or an animal that runs alone*
RUNT	*a cow or calf that is small*
WRANGLER	*the man who took care of the horses during the day*
RUSTLER	*someone who stole cattle or horses*
TENDERFOOT	*an inexperienced frontiersman*
VAQUEROS	*working cowboys of Mexico who developed the skills adopted by American cowboys*